I0815580

Intro to Russian

Bela Davis

Русский

Abdo Kids Junior
is an Imprint of Abdo Kids
abdobooks.com

abdobooks.com

Published by Abdo Kids, a division of ABDO, P.O. Box 398166, Minneapolis, Minnesota 55439.

Printed in the United States of America, North Mankato, Minnesota.

102024

012025

Consultant: Sarah Rosenthal

Photo Credits: Getty Images, Shutterstock

Production Contributors: Teddy Borth, Jennie Forsberg, Grace Hansen

Design Contributors: Candice Keimig, Colleen McLaren

Library of Congress Control Number: 2024936627

Publisher's Cataloging-in-Publication Data

Names: Davis, Bela, author.

Title: Intro to Russian / by Bela Davis

Description: Minneapolis, Minnesota : Abdo Kids, 2025 | Series: Intro to language set 2 | Includes online resources and index.

Identifiers: ISBN 9798384902867 (lib. bdg.) | ISBN 9798384903567 (ebook) | ISBN 9798384903918 (Read-to-me ebook)

Subjects: LCSH: Informal language learning--Juvenile literature. | Language and languages--Juvenile literature. | Bilingual books--Juvenile literature. | Language acquisition--Juvenile literature.

Classification: DDC 418--dc23

Table of Contents

Intro to Russian

Russian is spoken around the world. Let's learn some words!

Russian	добро пожаловать
(sound guide)	(DO•bruh po•ZHAL•ovat)
English	welcome

Russia
N
W
E
S
Belarus
Europe
Kazakhstan
Kyrgyzstan
Tajikistan
Asia
Russian is an
official language

один
(ah•DEEN)
one

два
(d'vah)
two

шесть
(shest)
six

семь
(sehm)
seven

три
(t'•ree)
three

четыре
(che•TEER•ye)
four

пять
(pyat)
five

восемь
(VO•sehm)
eight

девять
(DEY•vyat)
nine

десять
(DEY•syat)
ten

одиннадцать
(ah•DEEN•nadset)
eleven

двенадцать
(D'VE•nadset)
twelve

шестнадцать
(shest•NAD•set)
sixteen

семнадцать
(sehm•NAD•set)
seventeen

тринадцать
(T'REE•nadset)
thirteen

четырнадцать
(che•TEER•nadset)
fourteen

пятнадцать
(pit•NAD•set)
fifteen

восемнадцать
(VO•sehm•nadset)
eighteen

девятнадцать
(DEV•yet•nadset)
nineteen

двадцать
(D'VA•d'set)
twenty

оранжевый
(ah•RAN•zhevyi)
orange
красный
(KRA•snye)
red
цвета
(TSVEY•tah)
colors
желтый
(ZHOL•tee)
yellow
зеленый
(ze•LEHN•iy)
green

черный
(CHOR•nye)
black
синий
(SEE•niy)
blue
фиолетовый
(fia•LET•oviy)
purple
белый
(BEH•liy)
white

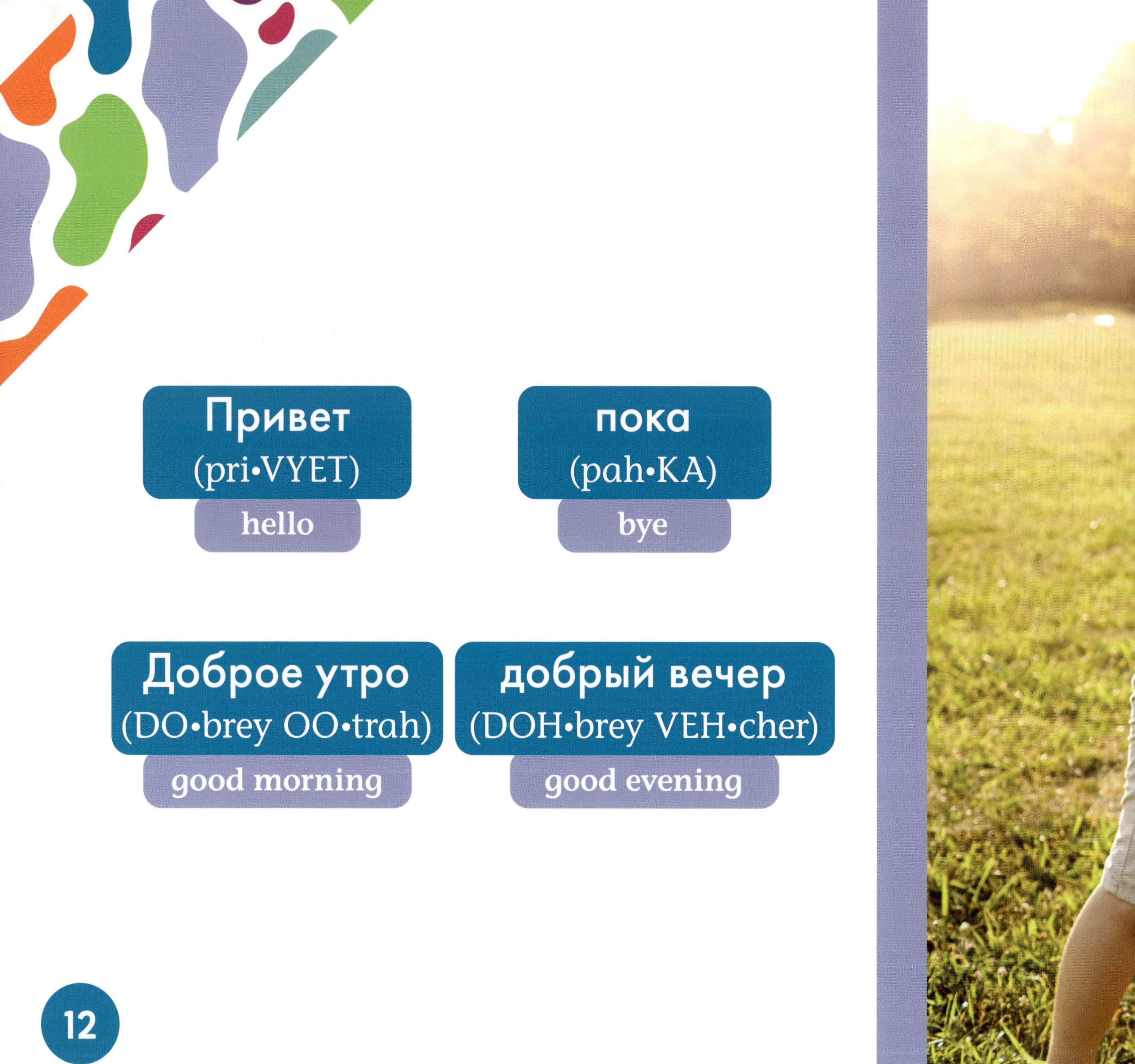

Привет
(pri•VYET)
hello

пока
(pah•KA)
bye

Доброе утро
(DO•brey OO•trah)
good morning

добрый вечер
(DOH•brey VEH•cher)
good evening

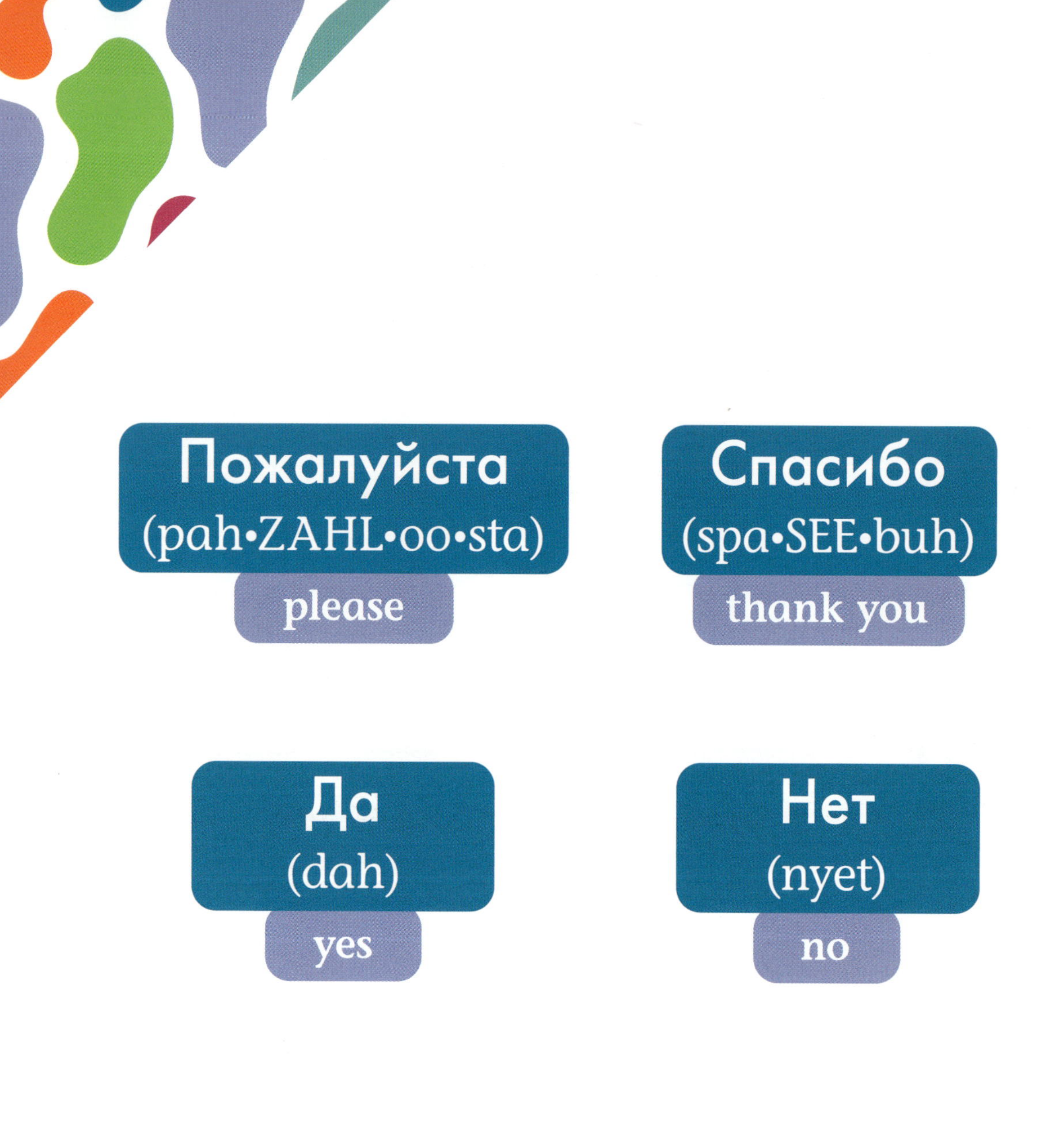

Пожалуйста
(pah•ZAHL•oo•sta)
please

Спасибо
(spa•SEE•buh)
thank you

Да
(dah)
yes

Нет
(nyet)
no

Crna čokolada (posno)
Pekan orah

семья
(sehm•YA)
family

мать
(maht)
mother

отец
(ah•TETS)
father

сестра
(sehs•T'RA)
sister

брат
(brAHt)
brother

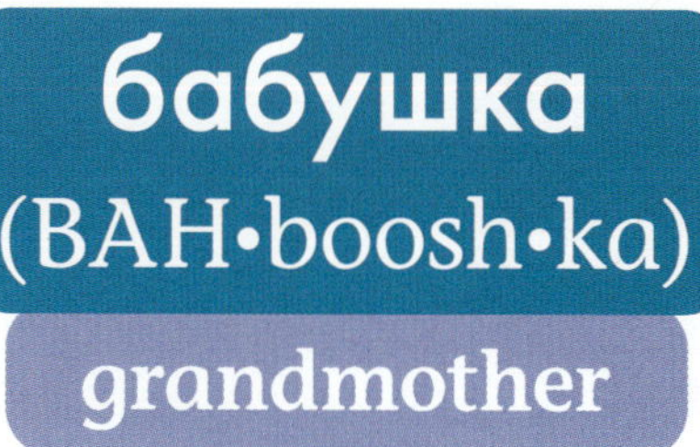

бабушка
(BAH•boosh•ka)
grandmother

дедушка
(DEY•doosh•ka)
grandfather

тётя
(TYO•tya)
aunt

дядя
(DYA•dya)
uncle

животные
(zhee•VOT•ni•ye)
animals
кот
(koht)
cat
соба́ка
(sa•BAH•ka)
dog

птица
(pt•EE•tsa)
bird
рыба
(RYI•ba)
fish

места (MEY•sta) – Places

дом
(dohm)
house

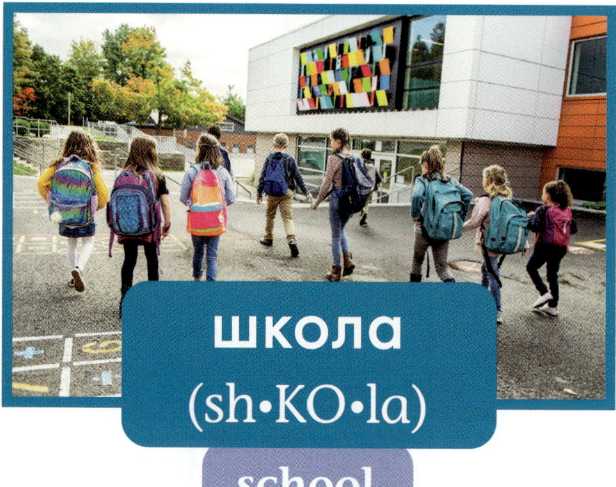

школа
(sh•KO•la)
school

парк
(park)
park

пляж
(pl•YA•zh)
beach

Алфавит (al•fa•VEET) – Alphabet

letter	sound
А	ah
Б	b
В	v
Г	g
Д	d
Е	e
Ё	yo
Ж	zhe
З	z
И	ee
Й	ye
К	k
Л	l
М	m
Н	n
О	oh
П	p
Р	r
С	s
Т	t
У	oo
Ф	f
Х	kh
Ц	ts
Ч	ch
Ш	sh
Щ	shch
Э	eh
Ю	you
Я	ya
Ы	y
Ъ	short pause
Ь	softer sound

Index

Visit **abdokids.com** to access crafts, games, videos, and more!

Use Abdo Kids code

IIK2867

or scan this QR code!